Superhero Superstars

# Gal Gadot

by Martha London

FOCUS READERS

BEACON

www.focusreaders.com



Focus Readers is distributed by North Star Editions:
sales@northstareditions.com | 888-417-0195

Produced for Focus Readers by Red Line Editorial.

Photographs ©: Jordan Strauss/Invision/AP Images, cover, 1; Shutterstock Images, 4, 8, 14, 16, 22, 29; Chris Pizzello/Invision/AP Images, 7; DC Entertainment/Warner Bros./Album/Newscom, 11, 19; iStockphoto, 12; Ysanne Slide/Moviestore Collection Ltd/Alamy, 20–21; Ariel Schalit/AP Images, 25; Warner Bros./AF archive/Alamy, 26

**Library of Congress Cataloging-in-Publication Data**
Names: London, Martha, author.
Title: Gal Gadot / Martha London.
Description: Lake Elmo, MN: Focus Readers, 2021. | Series: Superhero superstars | Includes index. | Audience: Grades 4-6
Identifiers: LCCN 2019054527 (print) | LCCN 2019054528 (ebook) | ISBN 9781644933688 (hardcover) | ISBN 9781644934449 (paperback) | ISBN 9781644935965 (pdf) | ISBN 9781644935200 (ebook)
Subjects: LCSH: Gadot, Gal, 1985---Juvenile literature. | Actors--Israel--Biography--Juvenile literature.
Classification: LCC PN2919.8.G33 L66 2021 (print) | LCC PN2919.8.G33 (ebook) | DDC 791.4302/8092 [B]--dc23
LC record available at https://lccn.loc.gov/2019054527
LC ebook record available at https://lccn.loc.gov/2019054528

Printed in the United States of America
Mankato, MN
082020

## About the Author

Martha London writes books for young readers full-time. When she isn't writing, she can be found hiking in the woods.

# Table of Contents

Wonder Woman
NNIVERSARY SPECIAL
$7

Chapter 1

# Wonder Woman

Wonder Woman kneels on a sandy beach. A fighter pilot is lying still nearby. Wonder Woman looks worried. She reaches out to help the man. Then, a wave rolls in. She and the pilot begin to laugh.

**Wonder Woman first appeared in comic books in 1941.**

Gal Gadot stands up. The water is very cold. Gadot squeals and jumps up and down. The **director** yells. They will need to film the scene again.

Gadot and her costar Chris Pine try to stop laughing. They need to be serious for this scene. But there is always room on a **set** for fun.

**Fun Fact**

**Gadot and Pine are good friends in real life. They have similar senses of humor.**

**Gal Gadot and Chris Pine have fun talking about *Wonder Woman* at Comic-Con International.**

Actors joke and laugh with one another. They enjoy making their characters come to life.

Chapter 2

# Miss Israel

Gal Gadot was born on April 30, 1985. She grew up in Israel. Her father was an engineer. Her mother was a teacher. Gal's parents always encouraged her to follow her dreams.

**Gadot attends a movie premiere in 2013.**

Gal played a lot of sports growing up. She also loved to dance. Gal loved the spotlight when she was younger. But she was not thinking about acting yet. Instead, Gal started modeling.

In 2004, Gal won the Miss Israel contest when she was 18 years old. That same year, she left modeling.

**Fun Fact**

**Gal has one younger sister. Her name is Dana.**

**Gadot fights as Wonder Woman. Gadot first learned how to use weapons in the Israeli army.**

She joined the Israeli army.

All people in Israel must serve in the army for two years.

**Wonder Woman imagery appears around the world in many different ways.**

In the army, Gadot learned how to fight. She also taught other soldiers. After her time in the army ended, Gadot returned to modeling.

A **casting director** in Los Angeles, California, saw Gadot's **modeling card**. He reached out to her. He wanted her to try out for a **role** in an action movie. Gadot did not get the part she auditioned for. But, a few months later, she got a role in another movie. From then on, Gadot knew she wanted to act.

**Fun Fact**

**Before she became an actor, Gadot was studying to be a lawyer.**

Chapter 3

# Getting the Role

Gadot was in a few smaller roles before she became Wonder Woman. She didn't even know she was going to be cast as the character. The audition was different from others she'd had.

**Wonder Woman is a very popular character. Life-size models have been made of her.**

**Wonder Woman teams up with other superheroes in some of DC's films.**

Gadot knew the director, Zack Snyder. He gave her lines to read. But Gadot didn't know the lines were for Wonder Woman.

Right away, the director knew Gadot was perfect. He called her two weeks later. He asked Gadot if she would play Wonder Woman. Gadot was familiar with the character. She was thrilled.

The tryout had been for *Batman v. Superman: Dawn of Justice*. But Wonder Woman has appeared in several movies. Gadot played the character in each one. In 2017, Wonder Woman got her own full-length film.

Gadot loves Wonder Woman. She thinks the character is inspiring. For Gadot, it's important for girls and boys to see strong heroines. Wonder Woman is someone everyone can look up to.

Gadot thinks Wonder Woman is different from other superheroes. Wonder Woman is loving and kind.

**Fun Fact**

**As Wonder Woman, Gadot often did her own stunts.**

Director Patty Jenkins gives Gadot notes on her acting.

She has strong feelings. She can be confused at times. Gadot hopes the character gives people new ideas about what it means to be a superhero.

# Becoming Wonder Woman

Gadot was an active child. She played many sports. She danced for 12 years. And she learned how to fight in the army. But she still had to prepare for her role in *Wonder Woman*.

Wonder Woman is from an island of warriors. The director wanted to make sure the character looked believable. So, Gadot trained six hours each day for six months. She practiced martial arts and horseback riding. Gadot also learned archery. She worked with trainers to lift weights. Gadot wanted people to believe she had been raised to be a fighter.

Wonder Woman runs toward a fight.

POWER. GRACE. WISDOM. WONDER.
2017

Chapter 4

# Breaking Barriers

*Wonder Woman* broke **barriers**. For example, it was the first DC or Marvel movie starring a female lead. There have been heroines in all the superhero movies. But they were supporting characters.

**Movie posters show Wonder Woman standing alone.**

*Wonder Woman* came out in 2017. It showed that superhero films starring women could be successful.

Many of the actors who play heroes in DC or Marvel movies are American. Most of the actors and actresses in American movies speak with American accents. But

**Fun Fact**

***Wonder Woman* was the first superhero movie directed by a woman.**

**A billboard for *Wonder Woman* appeared in Tel Aviv, Israel.**

Gadot is from Israel. She has an Israeli accent.

Gadot sees Wonder Woman as a role model. She likes that she can show a new side to the character.

Wonder Woman becomes more uncertain throughout the movie.

Gadot shows that Wonder Woman does not have to be perfect. Wonder Woman can have **flaws**. Wonder Woman starts the movie thinking there is only good and bad. But she learns that things are often more complicated. Gadot says Wonder Woman changes her mind a lot and that is okay. Wonder Woman is still a superhero.

Gadot acted in a second Wonder Woman film. This sequel was called *Wonder Woman 1984*. Wonder Woman will be in other DC movies, too. Gal Gadot and Wonder Woman will continue to show people new ways to be a superhero.

## FOCUS ON
# Gal Gadot

*Write your answers on a separate piece of paper.*

1. Write a blog post explaining how Gal Gadot got into acting.
2. Why do you think it is important for women to play superheroes in movies?
3. When did the first Wonder Woman movie come out?
   - **A.** 2004
   - **B.** 2017
   - **C.** 2020
4. Why might it be important for actors to train for their roles in movies?
   - **A.** Training makes them more believable to audiences.
   - **B.** Training allows them to turn into their characters.
   - **C.** Training means they don't have to work as hard.

**5.** What does **auditioned** mean in this book?

*He wanted her to try out for a role in an action movie. Gadot did not get the part she* ***auditioned*** *for.*

- **A.** trained and fought in the army
- **B.** showed off skills in order to get a part
- **C.** modeled in fashion shows

**6.** What does **supporting characters** mean in this book?

*For example, it was the first DC or Marvel movie starring a female lead. There have been heroines in all the superhero movies. But they were* ***supporting characters****.*

- **A.** characters that appear less than the main characters
- **B.** characters that do not appear at all in a story
- **C.** characters that are the main heroes of a movie

*Answer key on page 32.*

# Glossary

**barriers**
Things that make something difficult or impossible.

**casting director**
A person who connects actors to roles in television shows and movies.

**director**
A person who is in charge of making a movie.

**flaws**
Qualities that make a person imperfect.

**modeling card**
A business card with a model's phone number, email, and pictures.

**role**
The part an actor plays in a television show or movie.

**set**
A collection of furniture, objects, and backgrounds used for a particular scene of a movie.

**stunts**
Actions involving difficult skills or danger.

# To Learn More

## BOOKS

Hammelef, Danielle S. *Behind-the-Scenes Movie Careers.* North Mankato, MN: Capstone Press, 2017.

Orr, Tamra B. *Gal Gadot*. Kennett Square, PA: Purple Toad Publishing, 2018.

Scott, Melanie. *DC Ultimate Character Guide*. New York: DK Publishing, 2019.

## NOTE TO EDUCATORS

Visit **www.focusreaders.com** to find lesson plans, activities, links, and other resources related to this title.

# Index



**Answer Key: 1.** Answers will vary; **2.** Answers will vary; **3.** B; **4.** A; **5.** B; **6.** A